GOODBYE, BUT LISTEN

GOODBYE, BUT LISTEN

Poems by

MARK McCLOSKEY

Vanderbilt University Press
Nashville: 1968

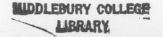

Published in 1968 by Vanderbilt University Press
Nashville, Tennessee

The author and publisher make grateful acknowledgment to the
editors of the following periodicals for permission to reprint those
poems in this collection that first appeared in their publications:

Prairie Schooner, "Goodbye, but Listen," XXXVI, No. 4 (Winter 1962); "My
Winter City, Where Is Love?," XXXVII, No. 4 (Winter 1963/64). **The Western
Humanities Review,** "To Him the Nights," XVII, No. 1 (Winter 1963). **Wagner
Literary Magazine,** "From the Ground Up," No. 4 (1964). **The Wormwood Re-
view,** "Love Poem," No. 6 (1962), reprinted under its original title, "Love
Poems 1 and 2" in **Best Poems of 1962. Nadada,** "The Sea's Reaches," No. 1
(1964). **Approach,** "Prothalamion," No. 48 (Summer 1963). **Poetry,** "The Smell
of the Woods," CIII, No. 3 (December 1963); "A Change for the Better," CV,
No. 4 (January 1965); "Our Kingdom," CXI, No. 1 (October 1967). **The Lit-
erary Review,** "Of Paradise," X, No. 1 (Autumn 1966). **Perspective,** "If I
Should Kill Myself," "New Stranger," XIV, No. 3 (Spring 1966). **The Fair,**
"Old Flame," "Sick," "Above It All," II, No. 1 (Winter 1967). **The American
Weave,** "The Father Watches," XXVII, No. 1 (Spring-Summer 1963). **Midwest,**
"Don Juan." **The De Paul Literary Magazine,** "Old Men Find Out in Arctic
Places," No. 1 (Spring 1963). **Radix,** "Those Who Go Away," I, No. 1 (Winter
1964). **Patterns,** "Poem," III, No. 3 (1961), reprinted under its original title,
"Two Poems," in **Best Poems of 1961. The Virginia Quarterly Review,** "To
Gather," XLI, No. 4 (Autumn 1965). **Podium,** "After-Funeral Tea," II, No. 1
(1967). **Sphere,** "Airplane," No. 8 (1963), reprinted in **Saturday Review,** XLVII,
No. 41 (October 10, 1964). **Epos,** "The News," XV, No. 1 (Fall 1963). **The
Denver Quarterly,** "The Shape," II, No. 2 (Summer 1967). **The North American
Review,** "The Movies," "Near Christmas," CCL, No. 3 (July 1965). **Quixote,**
"In Pursuit," II, No. 6 (April 1967). **Commonweal,** "The God of Light,"
LXXXI, No. 18 (January 29, 1965). **The Southwest Review,** "Whose Door Are
You?," LI, No. 2 (Spring 1966).

I am grateful to the Research Foundation of the State University
of New York for a Faculty Fellowship which helped me to com-
plete this book.

Printed in the United States of America by Curley Printing
Company
Nashville, Tennessee
Library of Congress Catalogue Number 68-17280

for Bernadette

Contents

I. Goodbye, but Listen

If I must go, do not be sad,
I'll leave my dragon with you,
For he shall guard your house
And burn your enemies.

When we climbed to the tip of the tree
And found the eggs were gone,
When we put our hands on the stream
And saw the sun slide over the rocks,

It reminded us of death;
And all I could say as we walked in the woods
Was that I saw a sorrel bring
A clover to his love

And rub her neck while the sun
Threw jewels in the grass.
Now that I am going, listen,
Let me introduce you to my dragon

Who breathes fire and is fond of daisies.

The Deception

Upon the chair I used
To offer you,
Wild petals have fallen,
Upon the shelf
The jar still full of stems
You spread in it.

My hands are not too sure
Of chair and jar—
Whether to clean the house
And make a fire?
Shall I go lightly out
In the drained leaves?

But twigs are not so dead
Though they are less.
I'll do something else,
I mean, than freeze
To rid you from my pulse—
Or think you gone.

What would they who'd set their cutting-knives
Aside reply to vagabonds who'd ask,
"Have you seen a girl go by this way
Without her shoes, her flaming hair undone?
And by the way, can you spare some wheat?"

And would some man, surprised at evening so,
As he was just about to leave the field,
Ask a vagabond: "Was it you I heard
All summer long playing in the woods,
While I was sweating out here over grain?"

What could that other do but lie to him,
Remembering how he and someone else
Had cooled their feet in brooks and taken up
The wild columbine for posies and at night
Lain in grass and taken each other's pulse?

But looks of vagabonds betray them in the end,
And day unties a dark upon the fields:
The harvester sums up his sheaves again
And turning says: "Yes, I saw her pass
Southward, singing like a wild bird,

But that is all you'll get from me tonight."
And then the vagabond embraces him and goes.

To Him the Nights

To him the nights are drawn out.
Under the moon that brews cracked brains,
He often flaps his coat, wish-winged, goes
Then bowed to the hill-rim to listen
One last moment to the tree-
trunks to find if they might yet pour into his
Cold whorl of ear the heat
Enduring them windy-lovely.

Often he has craned foot-
tipped on the highest rock, making
It a throne, and he the world's winged king, an
Icarus whose dare would not be melted
Down, and dreamed about a somewhere most
Beautiful abandon, soaring out
Past all his body could not do, because—
He did not know.
            The nights are drawn out
To him but he has always traveled back
With a kind of sad
High rage looking at the moon
Who never finishes the madness
                she begins.
He has returned to heap his hands with face
Between the quarter-winded walls
Where time presses him without looking,
And wondered what of king and hero he could get
Out of morning, looking at his up-
hung coat, his brain not even burning for the
Flat rigor in the sound of waking—

She, all sleep-saddened hair,
Mourning for the fire in her heart.

Ulysses' boat was black and swift;
Another, white and full of fish.

My lover said that Greece had changed,
No heroes left, no fine old rage.

What's wrong with you? I said to him;
If we don't rush we'll have to swim.

But he went right on cursing time—
And all I burned for sailed on by.

Now, for the first time, you leave,
    And I am here alone
Trying not to make the rain and wind
    Something other than they are;
    I give myself no time to grieve
But look for things to do and places to go
      To cover where you begin,
As though I were a storm and you a star.

But then there's night and being still
    Behind a shadow-door,
Where memories like flying sparks arise
    To make the head too hot for sleep:
    I see the way the wind spilled
Your dark hair and spun you round before
    I could avert my eyes,
And how at last I took you home with me.

Now we're whispers out of touch,
    And even though it's true
You did not run and I did not insist,
    I understand what darkness means.
    Perhaps you think the same and trust
That I am not so well as when I dwell with you,
    Having you to kiss,
That interlude is not as long as in a dream?

Be the earliest guest,
Catching her undressed;
Come an hour late,
Causing her to break
Stride; usurp a chair,
Frown at the others there,
Folding your arms; accept
Nothing her charm suggests—
Food or drink or talk;
Be the first to walk
Out, or the last; receive
Farewell silently,
Loving her no more;
Let her slam the door:
Stretch your hand upon
Darkness, not the moon.
Love yourself, the night,
Everywhere out of sight.

Not done with love, her arms
Poised in the air after him.
But he had left her bed and gone
To the door, open to the wind,
To look at stars and fireflies
In trees confused and blown about.

Did he know by then what dies
From lover's reach? He touched his mouth,
He rubbed his ring, but nothing came.
What stars had risen free
Of wind eluded any name—
While she, relinquished, blew to sleep.

To music cellos make, branches let,
In window-views, their summer go,
Beaten thin by sun their turning met—
Dazzlement that lovers know.

The violence of time's to meet and part,
This music seems to say—that fire
And snow at last construct the shadow-heart—
Swift diminuendo of desire.

So all I saw and heard you by recall
Suspended time to me, and dread—
The music that you loved and woods in fall,
Your voice, your shadow lately fled.

II. From the Ground Up

Out the groundfloor
Window, hand and mouth
Peeking at you out of dreams,
 I see you swing by the door,
 All spangles, all black hair,
  Braid or tide of sun,
An oil, hip in a white flounce
 Of silk, morning-fair.
 I, I see you and I
  Have spinning irises—
The bush beside the stoop sprays
 Berries up, a fly
 Hits the window like
  A drop of gold, the dust
Of someone else's furniture
 Of love, left out of light
 Years ago, burns, burns—
  And I am one with air.
But you are gone in a crowd of horns
 And dancing trucks, morning turns
 The lights out in my leaves.
  Still though I pull,
Lovely ghost, the shade down
 On spring that takes from me
 So much each time it passes,
  I have been fused to you
As to a priesthood in a wood,
 More than a dream, more than a kiss
 The red-bead bush and golden fly
  Crazed. For in this room

Your shadow danced, and all time locked
   In the frayed wood and all the dry
   Remains of love in those who held
     Dark sway of these walls,
Fired. If I pull the shade down now,
   It is to make you love.

I have seen mirrors visit you and salute,
While I have made them laugh and caused the chairs
To stub their toes and windows to pull their shades
And doors to yell at me though I have opened them.
And yet you have commanded them, and called me
Out of hiding; the sense I make to your hands
Makes no sense to me, and when you take me
On maneuvers in your room and make of me
A warrior whose armor won't fall off
Right away though you have begged to fight and lose,
Lady, what can you expect of green recruits?

The daisies in the window-jar bend to listen
To my guitar played in the dark, to my
Head awhirl for tunes to make you laugh and,
Running out of steam, whisper
"Oh that was great!" and say "Yes!" with your look
Long afterward. But what a crazy time it is
You're so bone-bent you will not dance.

Oh but love's a fine thing this way—
To know I cannot kiss you even a bit,
To have a fire spring in me and stay high,
Oh high, to think of giving you
A hat with daisies on it, or bring you
A glass of water with a cherry in it,
Or pick you up and throw you out the window like a kite.

Where does love go moonward from here? No,
I think it best to play the game,
To be loony in the window with a daisy in my mouth,
And look at you like seas, like grass in a wind,
And then shrug my shoulders, slump the failed clown,
And sit down in the window, waiting in your eyes.

It is morning again and the door
This time is stressed with trees
That overnight have blossomed leaves
And smells—the sunlight over
The sill smokes with odors,
And the red-flame cardinals sing
Arias around the walls and even
This far inland the blue tonnage
Of the sea is echoed.

They remember what winter is like—
Witches were scratching the door with their twigs;
And sniffing at the sun that leaked
Over the sill, he told her
The bodies of the last summer lovers were
Bones on the bare ground,
That crows were scratching on the roof,
Looking up their sleeves for food,
And the sea, far away, was edging in.

This morning when the door is opened
Her hair falls to the waist, its warm
Odors smoke around her eyes, the sun,
Rising up behind her body, fires
The edges, her necklace and pendants
Sway over the threshold, she moves
And the red birds flame up the tower
Of his throat and his hands
Open, and flow upon her like the sea.

Now they look out the door together
And see the trees dance in the wind,
Pitching their hair in drunken abandon,
See the sun roll surfs of golden junk—
Smoke of butterfly and bee—through
The hillock-grass, where the lovers rise
And look up, and the cardinals
Pitch their tongues of flame about their arms . . .
Now the sea, this far inland, is tipped with sails.

See no man that is not tall
When time comes for his marriaging,
Who wears his formal clothing like a king's
Gown, and wears the flower in his buttonhole
Like the medal victory discovers
Heroes with, his tall hat like a crown;
And walking in the moods of organ
And candle his parade
Before the smile of a kingdom
That has not seen the like of such a prince
Since legend told them how they all began
And what they hoped would come.

This man is a man like this,
But where the nerve is and the blood
Out of sight, he holds on fast.

Once after pausing in a shadow she had said
Him more tall and kingly
Than he could ever find in mirrors.
And in the church his body listens
To the organ, the candles and the gowns
Of God come down like water to the hand;
He listens, and forgets his mirror,
And walks, not looking at the faces
And ceremony flaming him a king.

Yet the nerve sizzles like a fuse
His heart would keep for detonating into skies
Of muscle—lightning or the rocketry
Of summer, when delight and fear
Go together.

                              And deeper still
He has a kingdom never left
Off being August where the hillock's height of
Grass kinned his hair and bounded
Him vantage to the wind to sail a kite
And shake to be so
High over river, higher than the cliffs
Across it. He had still
Some boy in him.

God comes down like water then;
Her veil fills out behind her like a river
Exploding sunward out of snow;
And he is black, like a pillar
In a forbidden temple in a grove
Beside a river. But even it
Shakes a little in the
Stone. It is a narrow step
To him, before the altar, on the brink—
Backward to the faces of the gentle
Believers—of yes, of yes.
                              Then in the water-
Smooth descent from ceremony he
Comes, collapsing with a smile, flying
Still behind his eyes a kite.
                              It is as king
They see him as he kisses
The women of the land and shakes
The knotted fingers of the men.

Her hand upon the bright sill
At rest, that seems much,
As if to know were but to touch,
Not as I have all day willed
It ought to be—thing
Past all figuring.

For I have sat here full of thoughts
On beauty's how and why and where,
Bemused perhaps by the April air
In other ways than young men ought,
Who still have subtle whims
And girls to trust them in.

But now to have in mind seems
Touching upon her hand that slept
For weight of my forgetfulness,
Seems that coming close may be
How we really are—
Though why and where be dark.

My Dancing Wife

Burn my indifferent marriage-look awhile
By dancing with a dapper boy,
My love, your long hair fire on air
The record spins, our half-friends struck
With your grace for the first time.

Let me who never liked to dance approve,
With gargoyle-amaze
Removed, your nakedness, my balance struck,
As all this farewell party is,
That you should have agreed to me.

Do not ask me later what I mean
That only virgin minds
Can strike their balance round a beating drum
Without embracing flesh, but rest
With me in envy's bright green eyes.

When bluebloods let their parties take
Those who aren't invited in
   (Like us, my love), they fake
   Their gaiety too thin,
And have to find an extra grace
Like the rouge for her scattered face
A widow must when the banker comes.
   The uninvited run,
   I mean, the risk of warmth
Making them more mendicant than ever.

But we're the strangers more than they
Who keep their hardest questions from us,
   Of course, and show us the way
   To the bathroom when we ask;
Who make believe they have to listen
To something hilarious when we examine
Their antiques too close and long.
   Our hands do not belong
   To us it seems, and hide
Like kings who have amnesia at dances.

We're disenchanted from the dream
That Paradise is a pleasure-dome;
   We traveled endless schemes
   To find our desires' home—
Such a place as youth could bear.
Now our nerves are prisons there,
And we can't escape the grace
   Of a stranger's constricted face.
   We find the wealth we wished for
Is hard for those who have it and bleak
For those who sneak the first time through its door.

We Weren't Fooled

We weren't fooled, and yet pretended
No cold lurked beneath the weather;
We left our house for night, my love,
And took delight in moon that burned
The hillock-rim, in rising mists.

We thought it good to court again,
Even though we could not go
Too far, stopped short by brooks
We couldn't cross for cold, and woods
Too bare to loiter in and kiss.

At length even the rising mists
Fell, and all that lingered were the leaves'
Stench upon the ground, the moon
No longer gold but white and high
As memory haunting us as we returned.

If I say a warm
Wind lifted in winter,
That icicles and snow
Fell shimmering to water,
Or say my spirit swarms
With light till aging grows
Very tiny,
What will you say to me?

You'll say it's very sad
That I have lost my reason,
And start to pry
And pick at your reflection;
Blinking at the looking-glass
You'll say no wintry eye
Can invent
A petal from an element.

And if I say who cares
If winter winds the clock
And age wins;
Now's the time to lock
It up, time to dare
Take advantage of the wind
And go to seed—
What will you say to me?

Without turning round
From where you stare at glass,
You'll laugh and say,
"Can warm weather last?
Don't you know by now
That fiery moods in the vein
Sicken the heart
Worse than a mirror's art?"

Then as always I will say
I've already said too much that day.

I wish our car were wagon now
With stolid horses drawing it,
To stretch the journey home out
To years, and wish that we could sit
Still in the frozen twilight
Where lilac shadows burn the snow
And light like rose reveals the hills
Highest up, and no wind blows.
I wish there were no reasons left
So clear that we should hurry to get
Home where we began to love—
That house our marriage set
A bleak interpretation on
When growing older hid the truth.

This twilight's where no passion waits
To put us in a wily mind,
For here through slow shadow-colors
Like whispers we can take our time,
And let our horses choose the way
Like history and alchemy.

Cleopatra's hair and yours, my queen,
Belie this wall of glass between;
The guard falling in love with you—his gun
And that archaic axe are one.
Must you sway your hips until his eyes
Make my death his enterprise?
Is it true our blood beats into dust
Who thought it had not entered us?

What do chairs and tables mean in tombs?
　　Weren't the lovers buried there
　　Stingy when they made their wills?
And when the time came for them to quit their bed
　　Didn't they forget a certain narrowness?
　　Darling, what do you think of this?
　　We're moving to another house,
And disarranging all our hands were fond of
　　Makes us lose our tempers with all the doors
　　　So that we slam them between each other
　　　And hobble round in wounded silence.
What happened to the gipsy-looks we had,
　　Seeing no good luck in settling down,
　　　In things that didn't breathe or move?
　　　Look at the furniture we've gathered:
How come we went so far we got to love it,
　　As if bones don't darken with their tombs?
　　　Well, it's enough death for us:
　　　It's better that we live on wind
And keep no dust or stillness anymore between us.

The Mirage

The street shut to traffic now,
Gardens without their fire
Of bed and lattice; every neighbor
Slipped inside his house,
Locking the door: none of these
Has made me dream of death.

It is, my love, that we have come
Closer than in April
When we were not so wed, so still,
But always on the run
Chasing the dreams we thought would keep
Desire out of breath.

It is the sense of you and me
Hypnotized by dust,
Of desert in the mind and lust's
Cool mirage that frees
Meaning into love—these
That wither me, that frighten you.

He has his mystery, and she has hers
To read in silence across the room;
Their minds do not depend on one another,
Outer darkness yawns and stirs.

From dawn their children taunt her hands above
All bounds of reason until they sleep;
His hand has had to shake so many hands,
It has no cunning left for love.

Perhaps a sudden storm will break the dark
And drive them to each other's flesh?
But lights would turn back on and they to light
Thrills, and vision leave no mark.

Of Paradise

We try to figure out with one another,
Tired of watching rain blur the window,
What can take the place of paradise
Since we have left that glaring waste.

For we could not pretend its desert brilliance
Filled us, like bathers on a long vacation
Naked on a beach, with blood-renewing heat:
A marriage has no time off from itself.

Oh we have tried to hug and kindle nearer.
Looked for others joined in hot abandon,
Scattering the rain. It even seemed
That there was almost sun at times.

But all have fallen out—and now we're tired
Trying to think out loud to one another,
Tired watching rain darken the view
We know was never really there.

I dreamed of getting you
An antique ring to win your flesh:
But each display in unclean glass
Was bolted fast.

I turned into the Square
And saw such water-bones adrift
Under the marquees as gave the lie
To knowing eyes—

The happy end in the dark,
The movie palace that seemed to lie
Open like its antique Star,
Lovely and far.

When I returned at last
In time to trance your flesh I turned
Away: best antique desire
Savor its fire.

Mark McCloskey

There Is a Girl

There is a girl whose wedding frightens me.
    The boy who shows her what to do
    Will touch a flame he never knew
Would take and burn him far beyond his means:
        Failing, she'll become
    A way to sleep beside a stone.
And yet it's sad she thinks it tiger-sweet
    To wed, so green she doesn't know
    Its fills the body up with snow
And frays the mind to walls and ennui—
        That she will come to this,
    The narrowed heart and the wintry kiss.

36

If I should kill myself, what would you do?
Would you come home from black and not remember
Where the doors and lights belonged?
The bogus prince who would approach and tip
His hand, would you shut your flesh to him
As you have always meant to do?
Suppose your distant relatives discussed
Your strange ways with strangers who would come
With straps and drugs, would you resist?
Would you disremember who you are,
And then in spite of leading questions be
Buried out of touch with me?
My love, I chart these likelihoods as far as morning,
But giving up beside your unkempt sleep,
I drop your hair and dream of other things.

〜 Mark McCloskey

Old Flame

Wintering now in tropic ennui
I wink at what I might have been,
I reassemble your perfumes exploring me,
Your ash-blonde hair and made-up tan.

I drop my wife's exquisite name for you
To piece together my turning out,
Sighing I've mislaid a tuft or two
Of hair, a tooth, a starry eye.

But such is merely drifting nearer death,
You would agree, I think, in the end;
Your livid perfumes chased me out of breath
To marriage vows, and so my thanks . . .

And boredom piecing you together now
To turn me by your brilliant style.
I hope you haven't grown cold the while
I've not been about to burn.

The flash of rip-tide and the rake
Of pebbles mix in your voice,
Turning thoughts in me as we go
Along the wind-shore. Late
Is summer, visiting is short,
I have no way to mend your secret.

But shift of what-goes and the lust
You whisper lift like a wave,
Brazing over me as you stoop
To pick the seashells. Once
Is enough, long ago I knew
I had no way to play your music.

I fail your patch-work and the tears
You wrangle out of your guilt,
Understanding this as you rise
Along an eyebeam: I
Am graceless, dark your beauty's pulse,
Scattered in your heart a lover's bones.

∾ Mark McCloskey

The Mannequin

I've promised her a dress or pin,
But going there forget:
Behind the shop a mannequin,
Dressed without a head,
Waits for someone to let it in;

Winter holds it beside the door
As though it always had.
I think of stones that have in store
Grass and flesh for time—
Zero bent on quickened form;

And think of death that waits in back
Of all parade and shine:
Are incongruities the masks
The mind spends all upon?
Oh even stone must burn and crack.

What do I love that needs a dress,
A pin, even a word?
And yet I know she'll have no less,
Despite this headless prop,
Nor I upon our nakedness.

Beside me, madame, stare without a light
At nothing: uncivil time has burned
Our childhood down, and slipped into the night.

Put your finger upon the pillage-worm
That goes to the heart of every king and queen:
Do not ask our rich hands to return.

I shall strip you, as you shall do to me,
And mouth to mouth and bone to bone we'll close
In passages so secret time won't see.

Invite all darkness to our lovers' pose,
All sweat, all blood. And now, my bitch,
How do you like the way our kingdom goes?

∽ Mark McCloskey

Encounter

Two cars crash: outside the house
Blinded by dusk
The man explains in circles,
The woman stares
Out her splintered window.
Whispers press upon detail.

Stanch the lady's wound, my love,
With ice. I'll tell
Our children pressing me
That nothing's wrong.
Come back and tell me both,
Misjudging distance, will not die.

And we shall not, my love, contend
Till morning comes—
You forgetting love,
And I that you,
Are not the dreams we dreamed.
Our children whisper, we must pretend.

They are so backward in this open room:
His children do not look at him,
They are too busy with party hats and horns
Of tin, and laugh as one of them
Blows out the candles.

Their backs face him in the summer room;
He sits in his highest chair beside the door,
Opened up for breeze, and watches the sky,
Blue for woman once, Madonna-wonder
When he worshipped love.

He wears his party hat too, his jester-
crown, sitting on his throne of upward
Ways, protector of his kingdom here,
Holding in his hand a horn of tin
And smiling at them.

He daydreams out the doorway at the sky;
The clouds are sailing there, grand
And harborless, as he has come to know—
And sky that has no color, virgin-blue:
He smiles through the door.

They are so backward to him and the year
Slides on the hinge,
The door is inching round upon the sky,
And he inside it in his chair, in the blast of horns
Of tin, smiles

Like the stiff man in his coffin while
The lid is being closed, and the flowers,
Big as clouds, pour from the fretted ceiling
Odors less and less upon his heart
Where the final drop of fire

43

Pinches out, the organ withers up.
He wakes up to the room. The candy
And the candles lie among
The wrinkled horns; the children have
Gone outside

And left the door a crack apart.
He does not hear them in the garden
Pretending that the clouds are boats
And that the sky's the sea.
But knowing they are there he

Waits for them and him to come
Back through the door.

Once my hopes were green and wild:
Now it makes me dark to see
Dust decline our dancing child,
You the sooner, love, and me;
Bones where the world lay
Open like a queen's gown.
Now I lose my sense of play,
Seeing my airy truths come down,
Hearing my shadow-heartbeat say
All's invested in the ground.

Still is it the same as death—
This bleak frame of mind?
Even though we must forget
All our once-upon-a-time,
Children really dance and play,
Wives and husbands really kiss!
Only say what radiates
Out of knowledge such as this—
If music of the beating vein,
If we can ever trust in it?

III. The Last Party

This was the last party of the year:
She, doll-rounded to the verge of wrinkle,
Took us in and told us to be mad—
Puff the lung of Cheer, blow
His cheeks like fire up
And liquor-ogle all the guests
Who howled!
     Oh summer is enough
To rob her from us—when she makes
Her long spinster-brooded dash from town:
When we return next year she might
Not be here, she may be with a rake
On the Riviera, floating with him down
The beach among a crowd of tinted glasses
And silken scarves, and laughing loud
Love? We wished it with a round
Of cheers and toasts!
     This was the last
Party of the year, and when it ended we
Would float like fireflies
Into the night, and she at last
Would shut her door and dream of maybe-when,
And how we slapped her on the back and howled
We knew she had a secret lover somewhere.

Don Juan

Money runs out at the ends of trips;
Freewheeling bottled me a quart of summer
Till what I plotted on my tongue to pleasure
Ran out on the cliff-high terraces in tips,
Shipwrecked in a waste of yachts. I sold my lips
To duchesses in boredom for the fever
The charts of their faces frayed from when the waters
Of love brought to their islands no bright pirate ships.

But when I smiled, it was moonlight to them,
And I became the shipwrecked hero on their coasts,
Heating them, fingering their brooches.
I let them tease the cork of summer off and send
Me maps of invitation to their beaches
Where I was whispered to the barns that housed their boats.

There were umbrellaed balconies that stuck
Out of the ancient buildings on the hill,
And there the girls shook out their flesh
In bathingsuits and touched their tinted glasses,
Lolling on the rails and on the stone.

And all along the fence the boys,
Whose backs he brushed by like a breath
They did not notice, hovered over,
Pointing and remarking with their mouths,
While the yellow bushes poured elixirs on them,

Opening their hands. He passed on
Until he took the hill-rim and discovered
The sun was much too hot to carry off
In his drumming temples, and he too weighted down
To pluck it from the peak it had and draw it

From the Azores to the North Pole of his flesh.
Then he looked back, and mourned the yellow latitudes
Of love and shook his fragile breathing down the hill.
But there was nothing left, the snow had covered it;
The white hairs on his head cracked in the wind.

The Girls

Are the girls I had in class
Having children still or making love
At night in woods, or in a looking-glass
Grieving for their little breasts?

But they were all a gipsy-band—
Arline-the-Sorceress who came too soon
To wicked children, wild-eyed Susanne
Just beginning, Pat-the-Boy.

And now that I have lost my hair
And mind a trifle more, and peek at spring,
I hope the poems I taught them did not scare
Their dreams and wild looks away.

For rage was all I had for them
Who put a spell upon my wit and made
My words a way to feel: I mean I'd mend
The hurt I may have done them now.

Everyone shall leave I know
(Those I don't really know),
Retrieve their handsome in a gesture
And back away from me;
Bagged in big departure's aims
They'll rollick off in rage and fear,
And I'll begin to hear
Silence approaching me,
And wave the harder after them.

The year is done in summer now,
Bees find the wounds in pears,
The dust that settles back to roads
Has made the sun a wound
That spreads through whirlpool skies in windows,
The lenses of departure's houses,
As I begin to hear
Darkness approaching me,
And fear that it will eat my hand.

I know men by departure best
(Those I have not loved),
For they will not remember me
When summers outnumber us.
Their houses have nothing left in them,
Their doors and windows rust and warp,
And I begin to see
Tomorrow approaching me,
And hope it takes me from this empty time.

Inside the magic ring their love intends,
They give their hands away, unclenching them,
And I, hot to enter there myself,
Can hardly wait to leave, concealing my own.

For they have been close friends too long without me,
And slipping from the smoke their greeting leaves
Upon my voice, I climb the hill outside
To lead me home through night to sleep them off.

Still that height's too black and mute for me,
The stars above it beasts' fierce eyes that guard
Its solitude: alone, untouched, I burn
My mirror up with me at length to keep them back.

I chatted with a man I wanted dead
—Who schemed for fans and girls as much as I—
And he with me: we put our darkness by
And put politeness on for show.

And so it was, face to face in rooms
Where fights were not allowed, where morning seared
The windows till they glittered cold and clear,
Dimming the black of winter out,

We spent an hour like some pale liqueur,
Steeped in dim accord about the loss
Of mild weather, the ennui it costs
Enduring sluts and sycophants.

If spring had raised the windows even then,
And on its green made hedonists of us,
We would have sighed and said we really must
Be off, and as we did, left each other cold.

Sick

My body's uncertain fever spreads
To dawn: shall there be sun, rain?
Ruin or Golden Age on earth?
Rising or long corruption of the dead?

But morning slides away to sounds,
To clocks that do not know of me
And instruments that can't record
What it is to taste the ground.

And so I listen closely to the sick—
The old who curse and girls who cry
Love to come back into them;
Children blown from fairy ships.

All are crossed in their largesse,
And now I have no heart for lies,
My mind's uncertain tenor spread
No farther than its knot of flesh.

I've told you now your map and book of God
This time I visit, father, are not mine.
Your smile is not there at such a news,
And you forget I wait to hear your own.

And now this room, lit up to feast your son
Returning from his careful distances
To tell you what he found out on his own,
Darkens like a hall about a stranger.

I wait beside the truths you made yourself,
My presence spreading like an odor in your mind;
You wonder what mistake you could have made
That I should bring corruption back with me.

All I want to know is what new times
Have happened here without me in the way;
I touch your hand and find it is not there,
And kiss you and rush off to a false address.

My Evil Genius

In morning's wilderness of light
Your tone of voice and touch seem
A boy I played with out of tune
And broke later in bad dreams.

For he had rescued me from boys
And gone into the woods alone
Where my green eyes tracked him down
And burned his venture to the bone.

And my fierce mind had been a king
To mirrors in its attic chair
When he came home with slain birds,
Prince returned from thin air.

Now my wilderness is death
That wears his face that pities me:
It is this dream your shadow holds,
It is your name I cannot see.

Two men can walk a long way at evening
Through town, descending the road's coil,
Criss-crossing it, one tall and young,
One short and almost old,
And talk of what there is between them
Here and there before they look
At their wrists to fix goodnight and see-you-then.

They do not hear the traffic, the children's voices
Fading everywhere; the taller
Tries to tell how far he's gone from boy
Without saying it, the other advises him
Of what he should expect from wily time.

They walk together; no one watches them,
And they become by dark and distance
No different in size and hardly two—
And linger in the same house for a minute
To drink a brandy to say goodnight the warmer,
Until the door passes softly between them
Where the road has coiled to, where quiet comes.

~ Mark McCloskey

That He Is Dead (for Cecil Hemley)

Below the hill, I see the same trees
Above his house concealing it.
Still he is dead, still the leaves shine
Before the storm enters them.
Tonight he shall invite me to a chair
Upholstered like the sea's floor,
And over wine and under the drowning moon,
Surround me with his brilliant soul.

The storm has done its trumpeting and fire,
And left my waking up its rain
That rusts and shrinks my child's toys and smears
Her stickman-drawing in the grass.
I go upstairs and stiffen into sleep
That closes me inside a dream
As something watching me among bright walls
But unseen though I turn and turn.

The dream is done when dusk invents my eyes
And rain falls to sharpened air.
The houses seem as through a telescope
Reversed; minute and sinister,
Someone floats away across the street,
Puddles shine like broken glass.
I remember now that he is dead,
And know that I was bound to him.

IV. Finding Out

Now it's colder weather tell
Windows to my thumb—the tendrils
Of the nearest trees to sight
Not half so ultimate with news
Of blossoming that slips, of warmth
Eddied away, as touching finds by chance.

And I wonder if I could know
By smelling it, if smoke
In sunbeams through the mesh
Of trees I dashed beside for reasons
Best known to summertime
Perhaps, could tell me fire uncovers ice?

And could I have heard in strong
Winds come to my rest
In a private greenhouse,
Ice, ice tinkling in the sky,
Or tasted in an oat's stem
The clear thin string of sap gone cold?

How can the senseless-in-love know,
Save by chance of touch,
What the leaves' glitter,
Far off to their busy half-view,
Meant, that where her wrist
Lay close a cold paralysis would lie?

Poem (for Willard and Marie Maas)

The end goes subtly everywhere
Drugging with what thick potion
Of odorous moonlight and the golden
Perfume of amorous bodies and dying flowers
The boys and girls, the heroes and heroines,
The villain with his odd teeth and stovepipe hat,
The nervous poet in his garden laboratory
Pounding flowers and jewels in his marble bowl—
Everyone and everything drugged and langorous.

It is nearly the end. The red zinnias
Once carousing in their circle of stone
Like the passionate heart in its cup of ribs,
Collapse on their stems like spider-legs
After the ruinous love of the royal moth;
Pears, over-ripe, now gold and streaked with blood,
Ache on the branch, twang loose, and thud on the ground;
A book of poems sighs open on the stone walk,
And a glass bleeds its red liquid on the pages.

It is nearly the end. We are all going
To death whispering, ripe with love, swelled
With our own golden loveliness;
Our children will be born into snow
From the black exits of unremembered passion;
Our hands make funny signs of farewell,
And our eyes are filled with the sweet smoke of fires
That climbs through the trees from the pyres
Of flowers and insect wings and floats
For a long time, like a memory, on the cold air.

The smell of the high woods,
When rain distills the night,
Comes to a house and waits
For no one to unbind the door,
But enters; none to fear the water
As ruin to the touch of things,
And shut the windows, but enters,
Indifferent to grace or fear.

And it will wrap the flesh of those
Who sleep or dream, who rise
Or have not gone to rest on time
To miss the rain, the high wood's
Point of loosening its smell
Downhill, into a house, numbered
By order of the man who owns it,
And her who treasures it beyond all measure.

I have smelled it too, the woods,
Dark and wet above a house
That love and I have leased to us
For just awhile, uneasy in it,
As given things we did not want
But had to guard, and wonder
If in the stone woods we have left
This same smell entered, and sleeps upon the bone.

⌒ Mark McCloskey

To Gather

I dream that after mowers fold
Their sickles up and wind through fields,
Disappearing in the woods at evening,
The wheat belongs to no one in its sheaves,
And that the last clear light above the hills
Beyond the fields is pressed away
By the black and blacker weight of distances,
Taking even from the eye its ownership.

And as I lie between the dark
Of sleep and light of waking up
Familiar to the feel of things,
I wonder if I've latched the door and window,
I fear I've left no light on in the passageway,
And know that as the moon becomes
The chilly eaten fruit of twigs
In waning, dark will have the house again.

Again the dark will grow I dream,
Opening enough for mist
To whisper through the door and window
And fall in drops upon the water in the vase
Around the withered stalks, retrieving them
To dust, the black and blacker weight
Of nothing sight or holding on
Can make a distance for—for thinking and for measure.

And then I wake afraid. No mist
Is in the passageway but light:
I know I've made the latches fast.
Relieved I flutter back and touch the hand
That lies beside me like a sheaf of grain
And think there'll be no nameless goblin
Come to snatch it up and eat it,
That I can see and gather it at will,
Even though I'll let it go in sleep.

66

My winter city has no ghostly guardian tonight
With winged ankles and a wand of snakes
To flit among the lamps and smoke a gold
Blur and ineluctably a warmth for touch
    By frozen hands, seeking
    Bright bedevilment.

My city has its silences tonight,
The far-off horns and mouldy bells that fall,
The liquids that reverberate in rooms
On nothing that can open to the fury,
    All winter-dark, all ice the rock—
    No sizzling at the core.

My city is a residue of snow tonight;
Someone has broken on the river like a statue,
Whose hands and blood are scattered on the ice
Like splintered rubies and a peacock's rocketry,
    Whose name is lost, and death
    No wittier than dreams by him.

My city's chimneys do not spark or crack tonight,
But smoke into the sky, smothering stars,
Deleting all astrologies that guard
The flight and bite of love's hot circumstance
    That said flesh was not stone, that said
    Cold hides a core of heat in all that dies.

~ Mark McCloskey

For Platonic Lovers

This year there is no spring
To confuse the mind, but pure cold
To sail through like a ship that tide and wind
Tilt from lush atolls at hand
To love's defended coast.

There are no heated days,
Though flowers tilt the frost and girls
Have taken off their belts and lie in the sun—
No burning days but rare and such
As foretell dead calm.

The summer's doldrum-press
Upon the mind shall turn the face
Back on foresworn isles, while rockbound shores
Mapped and set upon for truth
Seem too north and far.

And what shall lovers spared
Spring and pledged to strict estate
When summer deadens that resolve and green
Seems the heart of love conclude
But plucking out their eyes?

The calendar's a broken record of late
Of garden parties to attend and plays
Of comic cuckoldry, of deaths and births
I've scribbled anecdotes around in green.

And so it is that all the way from March
Gales to August's breathlessness I've seen
The young unroll themselves like treasure-maps,
The old paint Priapus round their bones.

The wintertime of sad and angry passes,
And for awhile yes won't hear of no,
The inconclusive pressures of the mind
Relax, and laughter glides in all events.

After-Funeral Tea

The charged, slow
Backwash of funeral attends
   To tea. Around the table
   Mourners sigh and yawn,
And lightly chat about their children,
     Of wreaths and tombs.

   If corpse's quirk
Of voice rises in one of them,
   He may shut his eyes,
   And sighing he is fatigued,
Pretend behind his cup he cares
     Nothing for the dead.

   Nothing comes
Of gathering in the wake of nothing:
   Survivors excuse themselves
   And hurry to catch a boat.
The rest is stone, cups, is
     Wasted breath.

You cannot get them inland where you live—
Tropic girls who dance for lavish men,
Paintings of a country dazzling in its hues.
Where you live cannot be visited.

Here the marriages occur in sheds.
The women lug their spring in wooden buckets
Before the men who sniff about their heels.
Flint and bone bully the summer here.

Where you live cannot be held as dear
As where you go until you go to it;
When all you look at comes into your hands,
Inland becomes where color was before.

You cannot visit places where the door
Opens upon the mirror morning clears—
The pile of flesh beside you, holding out.
Inland is where you come from and where you go.

An airplane, banking up the river north
At night above the city, balances
Those who make a point of ground,
A little frightened by the way the lights move up
In the wind-buck of the landing's fall.

It's the quiet that disturbs them most—
The bump of motors dozing off the wind,
The scatter of the city's lights
Without a creak. It seems a moment then
That they are dead, collapsing toward the stars.

Then they float across the ground. This is
The river, taking on and putting off its gamble,
Making reasons on its banks, lifting and
Falling as it should. Those who leave the bird
Forget the sight it gave them of the fragile land.

So they are down and make their way alone
To find the doubtless they are sure is there,
Lock the door and throw the lights around,
Then go to bed. In the dark, out the window,
They can see the stars the other way

Than on the plane, before they close their eyes.
Here conjecture doesn't happen to the dreams
They have of flight: their kind of bird
Has not been seen before, and lifts them
To a land of mirrors no one ever claimed.

Tonight, my love, dying tells the news
While sleep has taken you apart;
News about a famous old man dead,
And wails of children locked in walls,
That blend to beat and blow a frozen music.

I crouch here wondering the noise about me,
And why I don't go deaf in you,
And, as in a greenhouse, dream away the night
Where flowers do not say their honey,
Yet through their dark convince the listener.

It would be sweet to fall away with you,
But I am too awake to death—
Yield of the old man that my breath believes,
And closeted behind my bones
The boy who puts his wail against my wrist.

But you, my love, no news can break your sleep,
For it's as dark as when you pass
And old men see your shadow cross their doors;
As dark as earth which folds a seed
And makes it May whenever it returns.

Yet over what is boy and old in me
I balance, as on a castle roof,
While high behind me death drums on the moon
And blows soft wind-tunes down:
I'm too enraged against this ease to sleep.

And yet for you I could come down from noise
And gather heat and dark by you;
But I would not make sense to me so deaf.
Now while the news is bright and cold,
I seize my wrist to dare the beating end.

Mark McCloskey

Beside an open window on the verge of sleep,
I dream my death: could it be the wind,
Blowing warm through ice is everywhere
Below me in the town, has wakened me?

I am unnerved, but not enraged as once,
For when I used to think my dying out,
It seemed a figure with its back to me
At a party, talking to someone, taking its time.

In those dead days when I was still a dream,
I burned to make that idle guest engage me:
I'd have to lose, but I would have it loud,
Face to face, in terms of my own time.

But death is shapeless. Beneath my tepid breath
There's something cold, separating me
From lights that rise below me near the snow,
Their flicker holding firm all through the night.

I stand in line at night to see a movie,
Cold and silent wait with many others,
Wondering what's taking it so long
To let us in, and why I've come at all.

For now I can't recall the picture's title,
Whether it's of romance or adventure,
Who the star is, how much I have to pay:
But it is night and cold and no one talks,

And I begin to wonder if it's dying
Waiting presupposes, if that's the reason
Entrance takes so long, remembrance fades,
And I am caught between two unknown minds?

Perhaps I have been made to look for nothing,
Lured by lights like stars to wait and shiver,
Hemmed by dark? And what will I possess
When I have paid for death and entered it?

~ Mark McCloskey

The Farthest Look

What is where a hill is, dividing the sky,
Not where yellow puffs of wind consume November,
    But where the hill's thickets hover?
    What glitters there that smoke,
Rising like a string of snow, unbinds,
No boiling in a patch of prey or leaf
    It seems (for nothing human is
    In evidence devising there),
But something bright and yet a shadow's distance
White December in the woods will hide the more?

There have been runners to the distance before,
Who sent no news to listeners of what they found,
    But disappeared. The smell of war
    Has been a wind from far away
That makes a woman old before her blood;
The moonly face that loving turns away from
    Is close and clear long afterward
    To him who had the love's devising.
But finally there is a sudden death—
A farthest dark of lightness in an eyebeam or a bone.

My town has fixed these lights in lieu of stars
Above its streets, for wild song
Loudspeaker-carols in the empty park.
Those who meet by chance talk too long,
Until, having nothing trivial left to say,
They tear apart. In fields beyond my town
Snow becomes the residues of May's
Stars that hissed and flickered bad luck down
On lovers in the grass. A tiny beast
Squeals beneath an owl, and farthest off,
Where black horizons are and not the least
Whisper, the why of wild hope and lost
Belief reflects upon itself forever—
As if it asked for nothing, and couldn't answer.

A Strange Light on the Snow

The woods' and ridges' snow
Will lean to mauve and rose
By sun that ebbs, and all
Be stillness there—no fox's call
Snap the chilly air where dark
Comes to fool a hunter's art.

The road will let me rest,
And going there I'll fret
And hurt my view no more
In one direction, forgetting my door
And where my fears and reasons are,
Pointless and remote as dark.

But when there's left to light
Only the thinnest height,
And rose smokes out of snow
Like tropic dreams where women go,
Birds westward, swift and black,
Will call my journey's logic back.

Were I an ox or mule, a star
Or bedouin among his sheep,
Or Persian sorcerer, or sprite,
I might have seen you, Lord, a man.

But as it is I'm much too far
From origins like these to keep
Your memory alive. In spite
Of that, I do what zero can.

I make you bodiless for truth:
Winter's just begun, lovers have
Disappeared, my mind is white:
All is set for knowing you.

So come: I'm neither thing nor brute,
Nor foul and magical like man,
Nor sprite: I'm how you come to light
Confusing me, and so your fool.

"No more, no more!" I cried and left.
But there was no escape—wild Lord,
Even the wind had you in it and wrecked
All the craft my mind took passage in.

At least I remembered how to swim!
But lying breathless on the sand I saw
That I was where you forced me to begin:
The gull that slid above me cried your cry.

What could my mind do then but die?
You dove and took its splinters up
To build a nest—thoughtless how high
And rickety the cliff a spirit keeps.

Why is it these nights that moths
Shake at light till they are dust?
Why is it that crickets tear
Their hearts for light that isn't there?
Is it for light the midnight plane
Will not let up its cry of pain?
The God of light is pitiless
To let his creatures have no rest,
To let me want what they desire
Who fray against his net of fire.

Whose door are you?
Priest, spinster, spouse
Knock but to go,
Crying on the wind
Far from you, for love
Gone or never come.

Worms and stars renew
Light, tissue in your house:
They've the sun, bones
Taking their travel in:
Mind, however, proves
Utter simpleton.

But will mind's sheer
Want madden it,
Till it beat the louder:
"How can you be bread,
Blood? How can you
Open like a door?"

Only then you fear:
Prying apart our wit,
You contrive to enter
Us, your fools, instead.
Then, like wind renewed,
We beat at you the more.

1.

Lord, this season mends
Nothing of heart and head,
Sick for you; the dead
Heat of summer bends
Worship to utter shade,
Rooms where zero sits.
Come now, shatter it:
All the world is made
Numb with too much flesh:
Passion's need for wind,
Leaves' crooked din
Shaking the woods, fresh
Frost upon the brooks—
Fill that: I'll know you're there
Twisting upon the air,
And wear a desperate look.

2.

    Times must change, showing you,
Lord that nothing names, that nothing holds
        Frozen in poppy-wind,
           Waiting for me.

    Come then: words that summer grew,
Keeping the face of love from seeming old,
        Pledges petal-thin—
           Scatter them all.

    No, Lord, no don't delay;
All must be made sere and clear at last:
        Startle my poppy-mind
           Out of itself.

Let silence in stone and freshet say,
Stubble and frost in fields, birds that pass,
     You have not gone by
         Leaving me dead.

3.

So my mouth is closed
Awhile now, and fall is here.
Lord, let me suppose
You, for spite, no longer near,
And I, for pride, grown stiff.
Now no visitor will come
To talk me out of it,
All my subtlest doubts have run
Their course to heart's content,
And you for vengeance thinned the sun
To beggar's element.
So it is these days return
Rhetoric to dark,
Where you're the truth that twists and burns,
Fettered like a star.

It is Advent now, the mournful time;
Clucks of wooden bell-tongues call us
   From tying up the airy wheat,
     From golden, idle talk,
The merriment of dance at evening under lanterns,
     Kisses in the nooks of sheaves.
   Death has come to shame our hands.

It is Advent now, it gathers us
Between the four weeks of December's church
   To hear the year's demise announced
     In strictest testament,
To lay our prayers like wreath and vacuum
     Across the fence at light
   Housed high in its cold cup.

It is Advent when we daydream
Across December's flat shadow-fields,
   Below the wrinkled sky that blows
     Starlings like passion away,
When taking up an eastward view and hope,
     We pray that Advent falls
   And light's again invented in the air.